Ezra Explains

ISBN 979-8-89428-761-4 (paperback)
ISBN 979-8-89428-862-8 (hardcover)
ISBN 979-8-89428-762-1 (digital)

Christian Faith Publishing
832 Park Avenue
Meadville, PA 16335
www.christianfaithpublishing.com

Printed in the United States of America

Ezra Explains

Communion

Kamerin McCracken

Hey there! My name is Ezra, and I am here to tell you a wonderful story about a man named Jesus. Jesus was known for many great things. Perhaps one of the greatest things He was known for was sacrificing Himself for us on the cross. On this journey, we will see how Jesus told His disciples of His crucifixion and how He used the bread they ate and the wine they drank to represent His sacrifice.

Matthew 21:1–11

Jesus arrived in Jerusalem with His disciples shortly before He was to be crucified. Jesus told His disciples to prepare a Passover meal. During this meal, Jesus spoke of His betrayal that would lead to His crucifixion.

Matthew 26:2
Matthew 26:21

The disciples go to prepare the meal.

Matthew 26:17–18

While they were eating, Jesus took bread, and when He had given thanks, He broke it and gave it to His disciples, saying, "Take and eat. This is My body."

The bread broken by Jesus represented His body, because His body would be broken for us on the cross.

Matthew 26:26

Then He took a cup, and when He had given thanks, He gave it to them, saying, "Drink from it, all of you. This is My blood of the covenant, which is poured out for many for the forgiveness of sins.

The wine He poured represented His blood, which would be poured out on the cross for us.

Matthew 26:26–27

Jesus gave His body and blood in place of ours so that all our sins could be forgiven and we could have life without end.

Communion is done in remembrance of Jesus and for the sacrifice He made for each of us.

Remembering that Jesus gave His body and blood in place of our sins reminds us that no matter what we do or have done, we are forgiven, and the price of our sin has been paid by Jesus's sacrifice on the cross.

About the Author

Kamerin McCracken has been involved in children's ministry for over ten years. She has served in several roles throughout different areas of children's ministry from a volunteer, a youth camp leader and children's director. She has children's ministry certifications from the International Network of Children's Ministry and has a passion for seeing kids grow in their faith and ask questions expanding their minds and thoughts about God. Over the years of teaching children about the importance of communion, Kamerin decided to put the presentations and lessons she had taught into a book for others to read.